ENDANGERED BIRDS !

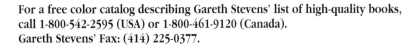

For a free color catalog describing Gareth Stevens' list of high-quality books,
call 1-800-542-2595 (USA) or 1-800-461-9120 (Canada).
Gareth Stevens' Fax: (414) 225-0377.

Library of Congress Cataloging-in-Publication Data available upon request from publisher.
Fax: (414) 225-0377 for the attention of the Publishing Records Department.

ISBN 0-8368-1422-3

Exclusive publication in North America in 1996 by
Gareth Stevens Publishing
1555 North RiverCenter Drive, Suite 201
Milwaukee, Wisconsin 53212, USA

A LOVELL JOHNS PRODUCTION created, designed, and produced by Lovell Johns, Ltd.,
10 Hanborough Business Park, Long Hanborough, Witney, Oxfordshire OX8 8LH, UK.

Text and design © 1995 by Lovell Johns, Ltd. Additional end matter © 1996 by Gareth
Stevens, Inc.

U.S. series editor: Patricia Lantier-Sampon

Printed in the United Kingdom

1 2 3 4 5 6 7 8 9 99 98 97 96

ENDANGERED ! BIRDS

WORLD CONSERVATION
MONITORING CENTRE

Gareth Stevens Publishing
MILWAUKEE

CONTENTS

Mark Collins, Director of the World Conservation Monitoring Centre.

In 1963, the IUCN Species Survival Commission, chaired by Sir Peter Scott, commissioned research and a series of books aimed at drawing to the attention of governments and the public the global threats to species. Sir Peter wanted more concerted action to address the problem of extinction. The first Red Data Book, published in 1969, was written by James Fisher, Noel Simon, and Jack Vincent. There had been earlier books that highlighted animals under threat and the possibility of extinction, the most important being written by G. M. Allen in 1942. The increasing threat to species and indeed our knowledge of these threats has resulted in nearly 6,000 species being listed as threatened in the most recent IUCN Red List of Threatened Animals. (IUCN uses different categories of threatened species, of which the most crucial category is Endangered.)

Knowledge of the conservation status of species is required so priorities can be set and management actions taken to protect them. The original Red Data Books were global assessments of species. However, many of these globally threatened species are found in only one country, and it has become increasingly important for each country to assess its own species and decide which should be listed as threatened. There are

Some of the many Red Data Books published since the first one appeared in 1969.

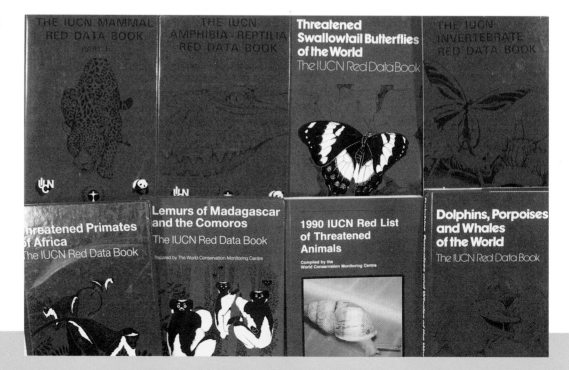

now many National Red Data Books covering substantial areas of the world.

The very fact that there are so many threatened species makes it very difficult to publish books on their status and distribution and, for some of them, we do not have detailed information. This *Endangered!* series aims to provide sound knowledge of 150 selected endangered animals and their natural habitats to a wider audience, particularly young people.

Our knowledge of threatened species can only be as good as the research work that has been carried out on them and, as the charts on this page show, the conservation status of much of the world's wildlife has not yet been assessed. Even for mammals, only about 55% of the species have been assessed. The only major group of which all species have been assessed are birds, and yet there are still large gaps in our knowledge of the status and trends in bird population numbers. However, their attractiveness and the interest shown in them by a great many people have improved the information available. Marine fish, despite their importance as a valuable food source throughout the world, tend to be assessed for conservation purposes only when their populations reach such a low point that it is no longer viable to catch them commercially. The 1994 IUCN Red List of Threatened Animals lists 177 endangered mammals representing 3.8% of the total number of mammal species and 188 birds representing 1.9% of the total number of species. Information on birds is compiled by BirdLife International.

The importance of identifying threatened species cannot be stressed enough. There have been many cases where conservation action has been taken as a result of the listing of species as endangered. The vicuna, a camel-like animal that lives in the high Andes of South America whose wool is said to be the finest in the world, was extremely abundant in ancient times but has been over-exploited since the European colonization of South America. By 1965, it was reduced to only 6,000 animals.

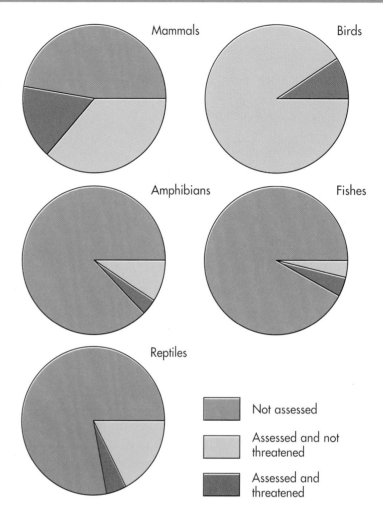

By protecting the vicuna from hunting and by establishing reserves, the population has steadily increased and is now in the region of 160,000. The vicuna is no longer an endangered species but is listed as Vulnerable. One high-profile endangered animal is the Indian Tiger, whose numbers had dropped to fewer than 2,000 in India when the first census was taken in 1972. Urgent conservation measures were taken, reserves were set up, and a great deal of expertise in their management has resulted in a population increase to its current level of about 3,250. Other measures included the halting of trade in tiger skins and other products such as bones and blood used in eastern traditional medicines. However, the other subspecies of tigers have not had this same protection, and their numbers are dwindling day by

day. Gray whales were also endangered. They migrate down the west coast of North America from arctic waters to the coast of Mexico and southern California to mate, returning for the rest of the year to feed and give birth to their young. As their migration route was so well known, hunting was easy, and, as a result, their numbers had dropped to only a few hundred. Since hunting control measures began, the number of gray whales is now in excess of 21,000, and they are no longer listed as endangered.

WCMC

The World Conservation Monitoring Centre in Cambridge, in the United Kingdom, has been the focal point of the management and integration of information on endangered plant and animal species for more than fifteen years. WCMC's databases also cover the trade in wildlife throughout the world, information on the importance and number of areas set up to protect the

world's wildlife, and a Biodiversity Map Library that holds mapped data on many of the world's important sites and ecosystems. It was IUCN, through its Species Survival Commission, that first established the World Conservation Monitoring Centre as its information database for species and ecosystems throughout the world. WCMC now carries on this role with the support of two other partners: the World Wide Fund For Nature and the United Nations Environment Programme.

IUCN — The World Conservation Union

Founded in 1948, The World Conservation Union brings together states, government agencies, and a diverse range of nongovernmental organizations in a unique world partnership: over 800 members in all, spread across some 125 countries. As a Union, IUCN seeks to influence, encourage, and assist societies throughout the world to conserve the integrity and diversity of nature and to ensure that any use of natural resources is equitable and ecologically sustainable. The World Conservation Union builds on the strengths of its members, networks, and partners to enhance their capacity and to support global alliances to safeguard natural resources at local, regional, and global levels.

Various organizations too numerous to mention help countries protect their wildlife. We urge you to support these organizations so the list of endangered species does not continue to grow. Your voice will be added to the many millions that are urging international cooperation for the protection and wise use of the wildlife that is such an important part of our natural heritage.

Headquarters of the World Conservation Monitoring Centre, Cambridge, England.

JUNÍN GREBE

The Junín grebe is a flightless water bird that lives only on Lake Junín, a 34,595-acre- (14,000-hectare-) body of water located at an altitude of 13,124 feet (4,000 meters) in western Peru.

The shores of Lake Junín are surrounded by wide reed beds where the grebes nest in colonies. Up to twenty nests are built 3 feet (1 m) or more apart on semi-floating vegetation. Usually two eggs are laid, but breeding success is low. The grebes are sociable for most of the year and live in small flocks. In winter, they live in the middle of the lake. They feed on fish, together with some insect larvae and crustaceans that are caught in open water.

There used to be several thousand Junín grebes, but the population has dropped rapidly in recent years to only about fifty birds. This decline has been caused by pollution from nearby iron mines. Iron oxides from the mines enter the lake from the San Juan River and settle on the bottom. The oxides poison the fish and other animals the grebes eat.

Since 1955, the lake has been used to provide hydro-electric power for the mines. This means the water level sometimes drops suddenly by 3 feet (1 m) or more. Fish and other aquatic animals are stranded and lose their spawning grounds. The grebes also lose their nesting places when the reed beds dry out. For a while, there was a plan to turn the lake into a reservoir for the city of Lima, but this project has been abandoned.

One attempt to save the Junín grebe involved the transfer of four birds to Lake Chacacancha. However, the birds all died. The only sure way to save the species is for the Peruvian government, the mining companies, and the conservationists to work together to stop polluting Lake Junín.

The only wild habitat of the Junín grebe is Lake Junín in Peru. Pollution from nearby mines is endangering the entire population.

FACTS

SCIENTIFIC NAME: Podiceps tarzanowskii

RED DATA BOOK: Endangered

AVERAGE FULL-GROWN SIZE:
Total length 13-15 inches (33-38 centimeters)

FULL-GROWN WEIGHT: 10.6-16.6 ounces (300-470 grams)

LIFE SPAN: Not known

The oriental stork is closely related to the white stork of Europe and Asia. It breeds in eastern Asia, from southeastern Siberia to northeastern China. After breeding, the storks migrate to eastern China, including the valley of the Yangtze River and Hong Kong. Some birds spend the winter in Korea, Japan, and Taiwan. At one time, the oriental stork bred in Japan and Korea, and wintered in northeastern India, Bangladesh, and Myanmar (Burma). The present population is 2,500.

The oriental stork is a solitary bird except during the breeding season. Pairs nest on tall trees in patches of forest set among swamps and marshes. The birds are nervous and do not nest near human settlements. The females lay two to six eggs. They eat mainly fish, insects, and amphibians, as well as some reptiles and mammals.

The oriental stork has become endangered because of habitat destruction, especially the clearing of its nesting trees and the draining of marshes and swamps for agriculture. As humans take over the bird's natural territories, there are fewer undisturbed places for nesting. It is also hunted and robbed of its eggs. Pesticides and other pollutants are another problem.

The plan to build a dam at Three Gorges on the Chang Jiang River will change the water levels over a vast area and may spoil some of the oriental storks' winter homes.

Oriental storks are protected in Russia, China, South Korea, and Japan, and special reserves have been created in South Korea and Japan. Captive breeding has been tried, but the program has not been very successful. This is because the males are often so aggressive with their mates that they may even kill them.

The oriental stork is a solitary bird during most of its life.

FACTS

SCIENTIFIC NAME *Ciconia boyciana*

RED DATA BOOK: Endangered

AVERAGE FULL-GROWN SIZE:
Total length 43-45 inches (110-115 cm)

FULL-GROWN WEIGHT: Males 11 lbs. (5 kg); females 10 lbs. (4.7 kg)

LIFE SPAN: 48 years

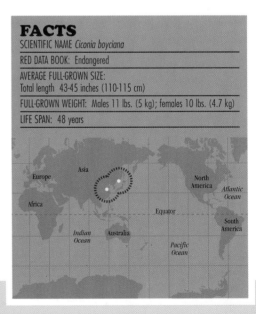

The greater adjutant is a species of stork that gets its name from the strutting military walk that reminds people of the army officer called an "adjutant." The bird was once common in Asia from Pakistan and northern India to Cambodia and Vietnam. It lived in wetlands such as marshes, coastal mud flats, and flooded forests.

There are only two populations of the greater adjutant left. Four hundred to five hundred birds live on the floodplain of the Brahmaputra River in northeastern India, and there are another one hundred birds in Cambodia.

The greater adjutants eat water animals such as fishes, frogs, and crustaceans. After the nesting season, the storks migrate to towns and cities, where they become scavengers that eat carrion and garbage. The birds used to be important for clearing garbage in Calcutta. The greater adjutant nest is a huge platform of sticks, 3-6 feet (1-2 m) across and 3 feet (1 m) deep, where three to four eggs are laid.

The greater adjutant has disappeared from many parts of its former range because the trees where it nested and roosted have been cut down. Some adjutants are hunted, and their eggs and chicks are taken for food. This is not a problem in India, however, where Hindus consider the greater adjutant unclean because of its carrion-eating habits and, therefore, unfit for eating.

A conservation program in Assam, India, is trying to save the adjutants by preserving their nesting trees. The aim is to persuade the owners of the trees not to cut them down. The program allows the owners to be paid to leave the trees, or the trees can be declared national monuments.

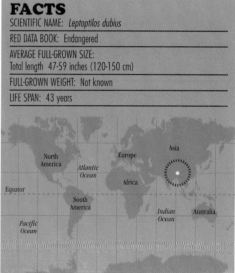

FACTS

SCIENTIFIC NAME:	*Leptoptilos dubius*
RED DATA BOOK:	Endangered
AVERAGE FULL-GROWN SIZE:	Total length 47-59 inches (120-150 cm)
FULL-GROWN WEIGHT:	Not known
LIFE SPAN:	43 years

The greater adjutant is a species of crane that can only be found in northeastern India and Cambodia.

WALDRAPP IBIS

The waldrapp ibis (sometimes known as the northern bald ibis) appears on paintings and carvings from ancient Egypt and was once found throughout central Europe, northern Africa, and the Middle East. Its European home included Germany, Switzerland, Austria, former Yugoslavia, and probably Hungary.

Waldrapp ibis numbers have been declining in all areas for many years. Until about a century ago, the species was still common in some places. But by the 1950s, there was only one small colony at Birecik in southern Turkey and a few colonies in Morocco. The Birecik colony is now extinct, and only 300 to 400 birds remain in Morocco, Saudi Arabia, and perhaps Algeria.

Hunting and habitat destruction have contributed to the decline of the waldrapp, but changing climate seems to have been a major reason for its disappearance in some areas. The loss of the Turkish population was due to pesticide poisoning the birds picked up in their food.

The waldrapp ibis is a sociable bird that nests in colonies on cliff ledges and feeds along riverbeds, sandbanks, marshes, fields, and other places where it can find large insects, fish, amphibians, and lizards. Waldrapps breeding in Europe and the Middle East used to migrate south in the winter, but northern African birds remained near their breeding places.

The Birecik colony died out despite great attempts to save it. Authorities and experts reinforced the population with captive-bred birds and purchased the feeding area to prevent spraying with pesticides, but these measures came too late. The remaining wild birds live in three or four colonies in the Souss-Massa National Park in Morocco. Nesting ledges are being repaired and extended, while methods of allowing the waldrapps to coexist with local people are being investigated.

The waldrapp breeds well in captivity. There are over 700 held in collections, and there are plans to introduce the species to Italy and Spain.

FACTS

SCIENTIFIC NAME:	*Geronticus eremita*
RED DATA BOOK:	Endangered
AVERAGE FULL-GROWN SIZE:	Head and body length 27.6-31.5 inches (70-80 cm)
FULL-GROWN WEIGHT:	Not known
LIFE SPAN:	Not known

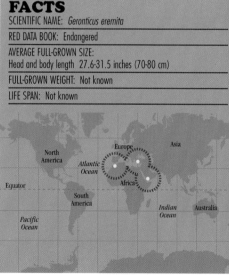

The distinctive appearance of the waldrapp ibis was captured in paintings and carvings in ancient Egypt.

This is probably the most beautiful member of the ibis family and one of the most endangered birds in Asia. It used to live over a wide expanse of country in southeastern Siberia, northeastern China, North Korea, and Japan.

Crested ibises spend the year at their breeding colonies in patches of pine forest. The nest is a stick platform where females lay three eggs. The birds feed in the surrounding rivers, ponds, and rice paddies on fish, amphibians, and invertebrates.

During the nineteenth century, the ibises started to decline because of hunting and loss of habitat. More recently, they have been killed by pesticides that have accumulated in the bodies of their prey. The only breeding population known to survive is about twenty birds in a small reserve in the Qinling Mountains of southern Shaanxi, China. There are also two birds on Sado Island, Japan, and a few individuals in captivity.

The remaining wild breeding population is closely guarded by the Chinese, but it is still threatened by pesticide poisoning. Since 1969, there has been a captive breeding project on Sado Island, but it has not been successful. A new project has been set up at the Beijing Zoo, and several crested ibises have been reared in China. One wild ibis is taken into captivity each year in case a disaster destroys the rest.

FACTS

SCIENTIFIC NAME: *Nipponia nippon*

RED DATA BOOK: Endangered

AVERAGE FULL-GROWN SIZE:
Total length 30 inches (77 cm)

FULL-GROWN WEIGHT: Not known

LIFE SPAN: 17 years

The only remaining breeding population of the beautiful crested ibis consists of twenty birds in Shaanxi, China.

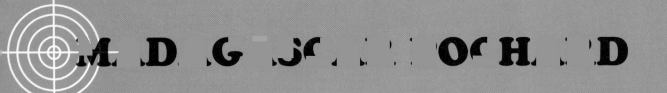

Little is known about the Madagascar pochard, and it may be on the edge of extinction. It is known to have lived only in the lakes and pools of the northern central plateau of Madagascar. The most important population was at Lake Alaotra, where the Madagascar pochard was common sixty years ago. One expedition alone collected twenty-seven specimens.

Since 1940, however, the Madagascar pochard has become increasingly rare. A few small flocks used to be sighted every few years, but intensive searches in the last few years have failed to find the species. The last record is of a bird bought from a local fisherman in 1991.

The disappearance of the Madagascar pochard was probably due to hunting and accidental drownings in fishing nets. The introduction of the black bass to many of the pools and lakes could also have affected the Madagascar pochard; these carnivorous fish eat the duck's food and kill its young. The development of Lake Alaotra and other lakes for fish farming and rice growing would also have made conditions difficult for bird life.

FACTS

SCIENTIFIC NAME:	*Aythya innotata*
RED DATA BOOK:	Endangered
AVERAGE FULL-GROWN SIZE: Total length 15.8 inches (40 cm)	
FULL-GROWN WEIGHT: 15.9-17.6 ounces (450-500 g)	
LIFE SPAN: Not known	

The last recorded sighting of a Madagascar pochard was in 1991 when one was caught by a fisherman.

The nene, or Hawaiian goose, has been saved by releasing captive-bred birds into their native home. The species once lived on many of the Hawaiian Islands before Europeans arrived in 1778. The birds nest in areas of lava flows in the mountains, where there are islands of vegetation. For the rest of the year, they live in open pastures on lower ground.

Nenes feed on leaves and berries of native vegetation. The usual clutch of eggs is four. The goslings cannot fly for eleven to fourteen weeks after hatching, so they are vulnerable to introduced predators.

The nene population began to decline two hundred years ago because of hunting; egg collecting; predation by introduced animals, such as cats, rats, and mongooses; and loss of habitat. The geese eventually disappeared from lowland areas of all the islands and became extinct on Maui by 1890. By 1944, the birds survived only in one highland region of the island of Hawaii. The total population in 1952 was thirty birds. Half of these were in captivity.

Since 1949, there has been a program of breeding nenes in captivity, especially at the Wildfowl and Wetlands Trust in Slimbridge, England. In 1962, thirty-two nenes were flown back to Hawaii and released on Maui. More followed, and over 2,100 geese had been released on Maui and Hawaii by 1990. In that year, wild nenes on the two islands numbered 555. They are safe on Maui because there are no mongooses. These carnivores must be controlled for the Hawaiian nenes to thrive.

The nene, or Hawaiian goose, shows that captive breeding programs can dramatically increase an endangered species' chances of survival.

FACTS

SCIENTIFIC NAME:	*Branta sandvicensis*
RED DATA BOOK:	Vulnerable
AVERAGE FULL-GROWN SIZE.	
Total length	22-28 inches (56-71 cm)
FULL-GROWN WEIGHT:	67.8-78 ounces (1,920-2,215 g)
LIFE SPAN:	Not known

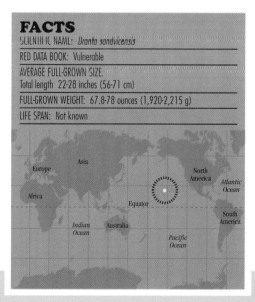

CRESTED SHELDUCK

The crested shelduck is a mystery bird. It often appeared in old Japanese paintings, but the species is now known from only three museum specimens and a few sightings of live ducks.

Records about the crested shelduck are scattered over a wide area of eastern Asia, including eastern Russia, North and South Korea, China, and Japan. It is possible that a few birds remain in remote coastal areas of Japan and elsewhere, and there is believed to be a population of fewer than fifty in China. They may also nest in mountains on the Chinese-Korean border.

Crested shelducks have been sighted on the seacoast and at inland reservoirs, streams, and marshes. Nothing is known about their habits except that they have been seen in small flocks.

Overhunting may be the reason for the rarity of the crested shelduck, but this is not certain. A Chinese forest worker recognized the crested shelduck from photographs and said he had shot and eaten two in 1984. As well as being hunted for food, the ducks are often killed for sale to private collectors.

FACTS

SCIENTIFIC NAME: *Tadorna cristata*

RED DATA BOOK: Endangered

AVERAGE FULL-GROWN SIZE:
Total length 25 inches (64 cm)

FULL-GROWN WEIGHT: Not known

LIFE SPAN: Not known

The crested shelduck is only known from rare sightings and three museum specimens.

The California condor is the largest bird capable of flight. It is so heavy it has difficulty taking off from the ground and relies on air currents to stay airborne. It once lived in many parts of the United States, but by 1800 it was confined to only the state of California.

Each pair of condors requires a vast territory of open country so they can search for carrion to eat. Dead cattle, sheep, deer, and horses are the most important food, but the birds also eat dead animals as small as squirrels. California condors are long-lived and only start to breed when they are six years old. They lay just one egg every other year.

California condors suffered when the populations of large animals were destroyed by European settlers. They were also persecuted by shooting, trapping, and the collection of their eggs. They died from accidental pesticide accumulation in their bodies and from eating animals that had been killed by poisoning campaigns. Collision with power lines has also been the fate of some condors in recent years.

By the mid-1980s, there were so few California condors that the remaining population of 8 birds was taken into captivity. With others already held in zoos, experts hope to rear young birds to release back into safe places in the wild. The plan is to build up two wild populations with about 150 birds in each, together with a reserve in zoos, by 2020.

Since 1992, thirteen California condors have been released into Los Padres National Park in California. Five have died from collisions with power lines and motor vehicles or from accidental poisoning. Another four were recaptured because they did not adapt properly to the wild, and the remaining four have been removed to the remote Lion Canyon National Forest. They have been joined there by another five captive-bred birds.

FACTS

SCIENTIFIC NAME: *Gymnogyps californianus*

RED DATA BOOK: Endangered

AVERAGE FULL-GROWN SIZE:
Wingspan 9 feet (2.75 m)

FULL-GROWN WEIGHT: 19.8 lbs. (9 kg)

LIFE SPAN: Not known

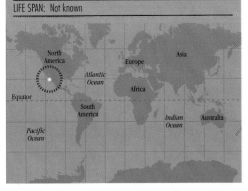

The last wild population of eight California condors was taken into captivity as a breeding group in the mid-1980s.

GREAT PHILIPPINE EAGLE

Sometimes called the monkey-eating eagle, the great Philippine eagle is found only on four islands in the Philippines – Luzon, Samar, Leyte, and Mindanao. It lives only in the rain forest, and its presence is regarded as an indication of the health of the forest. This is because the eagle is at the top of the food chain, and its survival depends on a healthy habitat with plenty of prey. Wherever the forest is cleared, the eagles disappear.

The eagles hunt a variety of forest-dwelling animals, including monkeys. Their nests are made in large trees, usually on steep mountain slopes. Females lay a single egg every other year.

The great Philippine eagle was probably always somewhat rare; the original population was about six thousand birds. Forest clearance and hunting have seriously reduced its numbers. There are about two hundred birds left, with very few on Mindanao and fifty pairs on Luzon. The numbers on Leyte and Samar are not known.

Although fully protected by law, the great Philippine eagle will survive only if sufficient rain forest is left intact. The Philippine Eagle Conservation Programme is attempting to breed eagles in captivity, but no eggs have hatched yet. Eggs and chicks are also being taken into captivity from nests in unprotected forest fragments.

Wild eagles are being protected by an "Adopt-a-Nest" plan that pays a sum of money to local people if they report an occupied nest, a nest with an egg, a chick, or a fledged eaglet. Through this plan, the local people become conservation officers during the breeding season and learn to value the eagles.

The presence of a great Philippine eagle indicates a healthy forest.

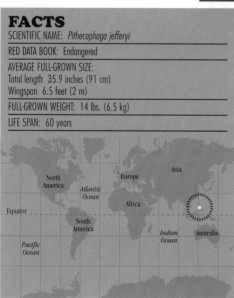

FACTS

SCIENTIFIC NAME: *Pithecophaga jefferyi*

RED DATA BOOK: Endangered

AVERAGE FULL-GROWN SIZE:
Total length 35.9 inches (91 cm)
Wingspan 6.5 feet (2 m)

FULL-GROWN WEIGHT: 14 lbs. (6.5 kg)

LIFE SPAN: 60 years

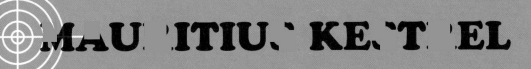

The Mauritius kestrel lives in the dense evergreen forests that once covered the island of Mauritius in the Indian Ocean. It is now restricted to the few small patches of forest that remain.

The reason for the decline of the Mauritius kestrel is not exactly known. As well as the destruction of its forest habitat, the Mauritius kestrel was poisoned by pesticides that accumulated in the bodies of its prey during the 1960s. The remaining patches of forest are also being degraded by introduced animals and plants.

The wings of the Mauritius kestrel are more rounded than other kestrels, so the bird is more suited for maneuvering than hovering. It hunts through the forest canopy or clearings for small reptiles, birds, and large insects. The nest, with three eggs, is on a cliff ledge.

In 1973, the total population of the Mauritius kestrel had been reduced to six birds, two of which were in captivity. A rescue program was started by the World Wide Fund for Nature (WWF) in 1973, and the species has made a good recovery. Three hundred and thirty-one kestrels have been reared in captivity and released into the wild. Of this group, 109 were bred from captive parents, and the rest came from eggs taken from the wild. The breeding of wild pairs has improved by giving the birds extra food and nest boxes. In 1994, there were as many as sixty-eight wild pairs of Mauritius kestrels, with a total population of around 250. It is expected that the population will rise to 500 or 600.

FACTS

SCIENTIFIC NAME: *Falco punctatus*

RED DATA BOOK: Endangered

AVERAGE FULL-GROWN SIZE:
Total length 9-10 inches (23-26 cm)

FULL-GROWN WEIGHT: 3.9 ounces (110 g)

LIFE SPAN: Not known

The WWF started a program in 1973 that rescued the Mauritius kestrel from almost certain extinction.

The cheer pheasant lives at altitudes between 3,935-10,665 feet (1,200-3,250 m) in the western Himalayas from northern Pakistan and northwestern India to central Nepal. It is found in patchy grasslands divided by scrub and wooded ravines and in recently cleared land where vegetation is regrowing.

The cheer pheasant has always been somewhat rare; it lives in small local populations where there is suitable habitat. These populations are sedentary, and the pheasants do not move from their territories. They are monogamous and are seen in pairs or family parties. The clutch size is seven to fourteen eggs.

The cheer pheasant has suffered from hunting as well as loss of its habitat to agriculture. The bird may be nearly extinct in Pakistan, where it is protected by law. There are recent sightings from only a few areas of India and Nepal, some of which are in protected areas. An attempt to reintroduce the species in the Margalla Hills, Pakistan, has so far failed. Like many other pheasants, the cheer pheasant breeds well in captivity, so it is unlikely to become extinct even if it disappears from the wild.

The cheer pheasant can be found only in the foothills of the Himalaya Mountains.

FACTS

SCIENTIFIC NAME: *Catreus wallichii*

RED DATA BOOK: Endangered

AVERAGE FULL-GROWN SIZE:
Head and body length 37-39.4 inches (95-100 cm)
Tail length Males 18-23 in. (45-58 cm); females 13-19 in. (32-47 cm)

FULL-GROWN WEIGHT: Not known

LIFE SPAN: Not known

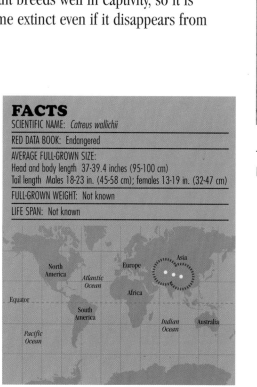

The western tragopan is one of the most colorful members of the pheasant family that once ranged from Swat, in Pakistan, to the Bhagirathi River in India. Its habitat is the bamboo, rhododendron, and other dense vegetation that grows in oak and conifer forests at altitudes of 7,875-11,810 feet (2,400-3,600 m) in the Himalaya Mountains. The tragopans move farther down the mountain slopes in winter.

The present population of the western tragopan is estimated to be 1,600 to 5,000 birds, but they are separated into small, isolated populations that usually consist of fewer than 100 birds.

Western tragopans are among the most arboreal of pheasants, and one nest was found over 33 feet (10 m) up a tree. The pheasants live in small family groups that are shy and quickly disappear into dense vegetation. The clutch is three to four eggs.

Loss of habitat to logging as well as hunting and disturbance by herds of goats have contributed to the decline of the western tragopan.

The largest population is estimated at 200 pairs. It is the main target of Bird Life International's Himalayan Jungle Project, which is planning to save the Palas Valley in Pakistan. Other populations are in protected areas. There are projects in Pakistan and India to rear chicks hatched from eggs taken from the wild and release them when they are independent. Unlike other pheasants, the western tragopan is difficult to breed in captivity.

The western tragopan is one of the most colorful pheasants in the world.

FACTS

SCIENTIFIC NAME: *Tragopan melanocephalus*

RED DATA BOOK: Endangered

AVERAGE FULL-GROWN SIZE: Head and body length Male 27-29 in. (69-74 cm); female 24 in. (60 cm)
Tail length Male 8.7-9.9 in. (22-25 cm); female 7.9 in. (20 cm)

FULL-GROWN WEIGHT: Not known

LIFE SPAN: Not known

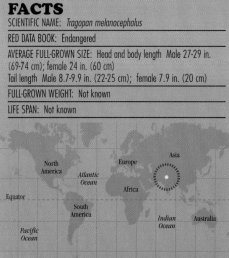

The whooping crane once nested in the marshes that covered a vast area from southern Canada south to North Dakota, Minnesota, and Iowa. Like all cranes, it is a long-distance migrant, and it wintered on the coast of the Gulf of Mexico in Louisiana, Texas, and northern Mexico. From the 1870s, the species went into decline as its breeding grounds and the important stopover sites on the migration route were converted into farmland. Hunting took a large toll until the birds were protected in the 1920s, but the whooping crane continues to be very sensitive to disturbance. Collision with overhead cables is now the main cause of death among young birds, and the Canadian population is threatened by oil development on its wintering ground in Texas.

By 1941, there were only 15-16 whooping cranes left, but numbers rose to over 160, including captive birds, by 1986. The only wild flock nested in Wood Buffalo National Park in Canada and wintered in Texas at the Aransas National Wildlife Refuge.

A breeding program began in 1975. Eggs of whooping cranes were put in the nests of sandhill cranes at Gray's Lake National Wildlife Refuge in Idaho, and the young were reared by their foster parents. These whooping cranes, now numbering six, winter in New Mexico. Another flock has been established in Florida, and there are three captive flocks. Altogether, there were about 280 whooping cranes alive in 1994. Of these, 140 were in the Wood Buffalo flock.

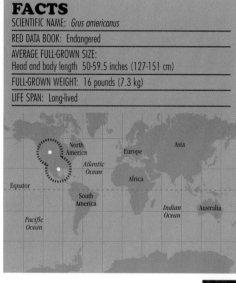

FACTS

SCIENTIFIC NAME: *Grus americanus*

RED DATA BOOK: Endangered

AVERAGE FULL-GROWN SIZE:
Head and body length 50-59.5 inches (127-151 cm)

FULL-GROWN WEIGHT: 16 pounds (7.3 kg)

LIFE SPAN: Long-lived

The migratory whooping crane is the subject of a major breeding campaign in the United States.

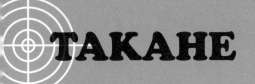

TAKAHE

The takahe is a member of the rail family of birds. Many species of rails used to live on islands but became extinct when humans introduced rats, cats, dogs, and other predators. The first live takahe was seen by Europeans in 1849, and only a few were found until 1898. After that, the species was thought to be extinct. Then, in 1948, another was caught. In 1994, there were about 200 takahes in existence.

Once widespread in New Zealand, the takahe is now confined to the Fiordland region of South Island and a few small islands. It suffered from predation by introduced mammals and competition for food from introduced deer.

Like some other island rails, the takahe is flightless. It lives in grassland and forest and feeds on snow-grass and other plants. Occasionally it hunts small reptiles and invertebrates. It is monogamous and lays one to three eggs in a nest hidden among grass tussocks.

The remaining population of takahes is protected by trapping predators, especially weasels, and reducing the number of deer in its habitat. Some birds have been released on island sanctuaries where they are safe from predators. The populations are being increased by breeding takahes in captivity and releasing the young into the wild. The closely related purple swamp hen has also been persuaded to rear takahe chicks.

The takahe is a flightless bird from New Zealand that is vulnerable to attack by rats, cats, dogs, and weasels.

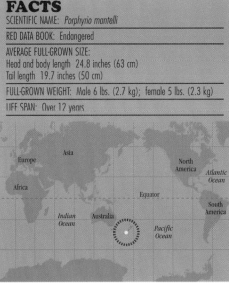

FACTS

SCIENTIFIC NAME: *Porphyrio mantelli*

RED DATA BOOK: Endangered

AVERAGE FULL-GROWN SIZE:
Head and body length 24.8 inches (63 cm)
Tail length 19.7 inches (50 cm)

FULL-GROWN WEIGHT: Male 6 lbs. (2.7 kg); female 5 lbs. (2.3 kg)

LIFE SPAN: Over 12 years

Kagus nest on the ground and cannot fly.

FACTS

SCIENTIFIC NAME: *Rhynochetos jubatus*

RED DATA BOOK: Endangered

AVERAGE FULL-GROWN SIZE:
Head and body length 21.7-24 inches (55-61 cm)

FULL-GROWN WEIGHT: Not known

LIFE SPAN: Over 20 years

The kagu is an unusual bird that is sometimes called "Ghost of the Forest" because of its loud barking calls. It is the national bird of New Caledonia, a large island in the Pacific Ocean east of Australia. At one time, kagus lived throughout the island and had no natural enemies. Since the arrival of the first human inhabitants, the birds on the island have suffered from overhunting and habitat destruction. The original Melanesian settlers hunted kagus for meat and burned the forests to make farmland. Europeans arrived in 1843, bringing rats, cats, dogs, and pigs and destroying the forest even more quickly.

Kagus used to live from sea level to the tops of mountains, but they are now restricted to higher altitudes where the habitat is undisturbed. In 1991, there were thought to be about 654 kagus left, 163 of which were in the Rivière Bleue Park.

Kagus are very vulnerable to predation. They nest on the ground and are reluctant to leave their nests. They cannot fly, although they can launch themselves and glide on outstretched wings when chased. They lay only a single egg, and nesting is poor in dry years. They eat snails, worms, and insects.

Despite being chosen to represent the world's threatened birds in 1984, the kagu has continued to decline. The species is being bred in captivity, and young birds are being released into the wild. But predation by dogs remains a serious threat. In 1993 alone, dogs killed 21 kagus in one reserve.

BLACK STILT

FACTS

SCIENTIFIC NAME: *Himantopus novaezelandiae*

RED DATA BOOK: Endangered

AVERAGE FULL-GROWN SIZE:
Head and body length 14.6-15.8 inches (37-40 cm)

FULL-GROWN WEIGHT: 7.8 ounces (220 g)

LIFE SPAN: Over 12 years

The black stilt now lives in only one valley on the South Island of New Zealand.

The black stilt is a wader that, one hundred years ago, was widespread through the North and South islands of New Zealand. It is now restricted to a single valley on the upper Waitaki River on South Island, and the population is only about sixty birds.

Black stilts live on stable shingles and gravel banks that form where rivers divide into new channels when the rivers flood in spring. Pairs stay together for life and remain near the nesting places. They lay four eggs in a clutch. Their diet consists of insects, mollusks, and fish.

Most of the restricted riverside nesting areas have been destroyed by flooding or drainage associated with dams for hydroelectric power, as well as by flood control programs and tree planting. The dry banks are also favorite hunting places for introduced cats and ferrets.

As the stilts have become rarer, there is an increasing problem from their mating with the closely related pied stilt. This may become more common as the black stilts have difficulty in finding a mate of their own species.

The New Zealand Wildlife Service has successfully reared some black stilts, and a reserve is planned for the Waitaki River even though there is little black stilt habitat left. Conservation of the species will depend on trapping predators and artificial rearing.

SHORE PLOVER

Shore plovers live on South East Island in the Chatham Island group; there are only about one hundred left in the wild.

FACTS

SCIENTIFIC NAME: *Charadrius novaeseelandiae*

RED DATA BOOK: Endangered

AVERAGE FULL-GROWN SIZE:
Total length 7.9 inches (20 cm)

FULL-GROWN WEIGHT: 2.1 ounces (60 g)

LIFE SPAN: 17 years

When Europeans first settled in New Zealand, the shore plover could be found around the coasts of North and South islands and on the Chatham Islands lying to the east of New Zealand. It was a very tame bird and soon fell prey to introduced predators, such as cats and rats. By 1880, it was already very rare, and twenty years later it was extinct on North and South islands and had disappeared from many of the Chatham Islands.

The last sanctuary of the shore plover was South East Island. Although there were no cats or rats on this island, the species was still not safe because birds and their eggs were collected as specimens. By 1937, there were only seventy pairs.

The shore plover nests on beaches, laying its three eggs in a nest hidden under vegetation or boulders. It feeds on any small animals it can find near the shoreline. Outside the breeding season, shore plovers live in flocks, but they do not migrate.

The population rose to 120 birds in 1985, but only forty pairs bred. This was because sheep and cattle were removed from the islands, allowing the grass to grow long and making it difficult for the shore plovers to find food. In 1993, there were 106 adults.

Shore plovers are safe on South East Island, provided predators are not introduced. To make the population safer, some birds were taken to Mangere Island, another rat- and cat-free island in the Chatham Islands, but they flew back to South East Island. A captive population has now been established at the National Wildlife Centre, Mount Bruce, North Island. Shore plovers will be taken from there to establish new colonies on safe islands around New Zealand.

ESKIMO CURLEW

An artist's impression of Eskimo curlews. Once common birds, they are now so rare that the entire world population is probably between twenty and fifty birds.

Eskimo curlews were once so numerous they were called "prairie pigeons," because the huge migrating flocks were like swarms of passenger pigeons. Passenger pigeons are now extinct, and Eskimo curlews are not far behind.

Eskimo curlews nested in the Northwest Territories of Canada and perhaps in Alaska, and they migrated for the winter to the pampas grasslands of southern South America, from southern Brazil to Argentina.

On the autumn migration, so many Eskimo curlews were shot as they passed down the New England coast that their bodies were collected by the cartload. When they flew north again, they passed through Central America and over the plains and prairies of the midwestern United States, where they met more organized hunting. They also suffered from the habitat destruction of their wintering grounds and on migration stopover sites.

The Eskimo curlew was declining in the 1870s and had almost disappeared in the 1890s. One was seen in Texas in 1945, then another in 1959. Since then, there have been regular reports, including birds seen on the breeding grounds. The entire population is probably only twenty to fifty birds.

Plans have been made to help the Eskimo curlew by captive breeding. However, the failure of numbers to rise, despite the lack of hunting in recent years, suggests that there is also an ecological problem affecting the species. If this is the case, nothing can help it survive.

The pink pigeon lives only on the island of Mauritius, where it has been rare for 150 years. Even one hundred years ago, it was believed to be heading for extinction, and the population has been critically low since 1960. The original home of pink pigeons was in evergreen forest and scrubland that survives only in patches. The last population lived in a wood of introduced Japanese red cedar.

Pink pigeons feed mainly in the canopy of trees where they eat leaves, flowers, and fruit, but they also come to the ground to feed on small animals. The clutch is one or two eggs, and breeding success is low.

Pink pigeon flesh was once thought to be poisonous, so the pigeons were not hunted, but they are attacked by introduced monkeys and rats. Habitat destruction has been very serious, especially when the island is hit by cyclones that kill the pigeons and destroy their food.

In 1984, there were only fifteen to twenty birds in the wild, but ninety to one hundred lived in captivity. Captive-bred pigeons have been released in selected areas of Mauritius, such as the Royal Botanic Gardens at Pamplemousses and the original red cedar forest. Such sites are either free of predators or have predator-control programs. Red cedars are being planted to provide nesting places. There were over fifty free-living pink pigeons in 1994, and experts hope to build up a population of at least two hundred.

Active steps are being taken to enlarge the wild population of the pink pigeon of Mauritius.

FACTS

SCIENTIFIC NAME: *Columba mayeri*

RED DATA BOOK: Endangered

AVERAGE FULL-GROWN SIZE:
Head and body length 12.6 inches (32 cm)

FULL-GROWN WEIGHT: 12.3 ounces (350 g)

LIFE SPAN: Not known

PHILIPPINE COCKATOO

Fifty years ago, the Philippine cockatoo was considered a common bird and could be seen on most of the islands in the Philippines. It lives on the edges of forests and mangrove swamps and comes out to raid maize crops.

Philippine cockatoos nest in tall trees and lay two eggs. Many pairs roost near their nests, but others fly to tall coconut trees on undisturbed islands. They eat fruit, nuts, and seeds.

Loss of lowland forest and mangrove swamps has robbed the Philippine cockatoo of its habitat. Now that there are only 1,000 to 4,000 cockatoos left, capture for the cage bird trade is probably the most serious threat to the species. Collectors rob the nests of all the nestlings and the adult in attendance. Another problem is that a high proportion of Philippine cockatoos suffers from aspergillosis, a fungus disease. They inhale the spores of the fungus, which lives in their nests.

The Philippine cockatoo lives in the St. Pauls Subterranean National Park and on the island of Palawan, which is a game reserve where it is illegal to catch wild animals. If these protected areas are effective, the species will be safe from trappers. Although over three hundred birds are held in captivity, breeding has rarely been successful, and many captive birds die.

The Philippine cockatoo is under threat from the world's illegal cage bird trade.

FACTS

SCIENTIFIC NAME: *Cacatua haematuropygia*

RED DATA BOOK: Endangered

AVERAGE FULL-GROWN SIZE:
Total length 12.2 inches (31 cm)

FULL-GROWN WEIGHT: 10.2 ounces (288 g)

LIFE SPAN: Not known

The salmon-crested cockatoo lives in the forests of the islands of Seram, Saparua, and Hauku in the southern Moluccas, in Indonesia. It has also been introduced to the neighboring island of Ambon. It was once common, especially in primary forests, although it survived in smaller numbers in forests that had recently been logged. There are less than eight thousand individuals left, and the numbers are declining.

Outside the breeding season, salmon-crested cockatoos live in flocks. Nests are made in hollow trees, and females lay two eggs. The birds eat seeds, nuts, and berries, and possibly insects. The cockatoos raid coconut plantations and attack young coconuts by chewing through the husks to get at the milk.

Although logging of the forests reduces the numbers of salmon-crested cockatoos, the main threat is the cage bird trade. When there was a proposal to ban trade in the species, there was a rush to buy up salmon-crested cockatoos while export was still legal. As many as five thousand cockatoos were bought and sold in some years before the ban came into effect in 1989. A survey showed that the species was rare or absent in areas of suitable habitat, which suggests it had been removed by collectors. Despite the complete ban on trade, birds can still be found in markets.

Over three hundred salmon-crested cockatoos are held in zoos, and there are probably more than ten thousand in private collections. Unfortunately, the species does not breed as well in captivity as some other cockatoos.

The salmon-crested cockatoo is beautiful and valuable.

FACTS

SCIENTIFIC NAME: *Cacatua moluccensis*

RED DATA BOOK: Endangered

AVERAGE FULL-GROWN SIZE:
Head and body length 20.5 inches (52 cm)

FULL-GROWN WEIGHT: Not known

LIFE SPAN: Not known

IMPERIAL PARROT

This is the most spectacular of the Amazon parrots, and it lives only on the island of Dominica in the West Indies. It is confined to rain forests on the mountain slopes of Morne Diablotin in the northern region of the island.

Experts once thought the imperial parrot would be safe in the dense forests that were so remote and inaccessible that hunters could not penetrate them and timber companies could not extract logs. However, the parrots have been retreating up the mountain as their habitat has disappeared. Estimates in 1993 claimed there were only eighty to one hundred imperial parrots left in the wild, but more recent observations suggest there may be more.

Although habitat destruction limited the areas of forest where parrots lived, hunting reduced their numbers even when there was habitat available. Imperial parrots were traditionally killed for food, but they were also hunted for the pet trade. Twenty years ago, this was as great a threat as habitat destruction. Imperial parrots are now protected by law, and trade in captive birds is banned. Some parrots are still captured illegally, but this is probably not a serious threat.

Dominica suffers from hurricanes that sweep across the island, blowing down trees and killing birds. Hurricane David caused great destruction in 1979. Parrots were killed, and the fruits that are their main food were destroyed. Furthermore, the destruction of forests makes it easier to clear the land for cultivation and allows hunters to find animals to kill.

Imperial parrots lay only two eggs and usually rear one chick from them, every other year. Conservation efforts will, therefore, take a long time to show success. Conservation needs habitat preservation, prevention of live parrot smuggling, and the education of local people about the importance of the imperial parrot.

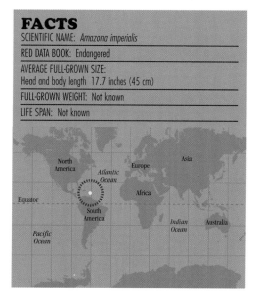

FACTS

SCIENTIFIC NAME:	*Amazona imperialis*
RED DATA BOOK:	Endangered
AVERAGE FULL-GROWN SIZE: Head and body length 17.7 inches (45 cm)	
FULL-GROWN WEIGHT:	Not known
LIFE SPAN:	Not known

The imperial parrot may be more common than once thought, but it is still endangered.

When Christopher Columbus sailed to Puerto Rico in 1493, there were hundreds of thousands of Puerto Rican parrots living on the island. They lived in the forests that clothed the island, but those forests have almost completely disappeared. The human population has grown rapidly in the last hundred or so years, and destruction of the forest has increased as a result. In 1975, there were only thirteen Puerto Rican parrots left in the wild. All live in the remaining 3,955 acres (1,600 hectares) of rain forest in the Luquillo Mountains.

Puerto Rican parrots feed on fruit, with some leaves and flowers. Flocks of parrots sometimes attack crops, which has led to their persecution. Nests are made in natural holes in trees or cliffs. The favorite nesting tree is the palo colorado. Females lay two to four eggs.

As well as from the loss of their forest home, Puerto Rican parrots suffer from many other threats. Large numbers have been caught for sale as cage birds. Introduced honeybees take over their nest holes, and the trees may then be cut down so humans can get the honey. Birds called pearly-eyed thrashers also take over the nests. Predation by hawks is a serious problem for the small remaining parrot population.

Conservation efforts include patrolling the Luquillo Mountains to prevent hunting and capture of the parrots. Conservationists have taken action to reduce the numbers of thrashers. They have improved the nest holes by making them deeper and well drained, and by modifying the entrances so predators cannot get in. Captive breeding was started in 1970. There are now over fifty parrots in captivity, and some have even been released.

The wild population of Puerto Rican parrots is still very small. It had increased to forty-seven in 1989, but Hurricane Hugo struck the Luquillo Mountains in that year, and half the population was lost. Old trees with holes suitable for nesting are very vulnerable to hurricanes, and very few are still standing.

An artist's impression of Puerto Rican parrots in their natural habitat. There may be only about twenty birds left in the wild.

FACTS

SCIENTIFIC NAME:	*Amazona vittata*
RED DATA BOOK:	Endangered
AVERAGE FULL-GROWN SIZE: Total length 11.8 inches (30 cm)	
FULL-GROWN WEIGHT: 8.8–10.6 ounces (250–300 g)	
LIFE SPAN: Not known	

Although the blue-throated macaw has been known for over one hundred years, it is a mystery to ornithologists. Until recently, almost all that was known about it came from hunters and dealers in the cage bird trade. They were catching and selling blue-throated macaws when ornithologists did not even know where the birds lived. Experts now know that the blue-throated macaw lives in Beni, a region of northern Bolivia, and perhaps two other places. Its habitat consists of scattered clumps of trees in the savanna and of forests that line the banks of rivers and lakes.

Blue-throated macaws live in pairs or small flocks, often associating with flocks of blue-and-yellow macaws. Their favorite food is palm nuts, but they also eat seeds and fruit. According to hunters, nests are in holes in trees, and females lay two eggs.

It is probable that the blue-throated macaw has never been abundant, but there are now probably less than one thousand. Because of their rarity, they are specially sought by cage bird dealers. Local hunters know they can get a better price than for more common species.

International trade in blue-throated macaws is banned, and they are a protected species in Bolivia. They are also protected by their remote habitat. However, trade continues by smuggling. Legally exported parrots must be examined carefully, because blue-throated macaws are sometimes painted by smugglers so they look like the similar blue-and-yellow macaws.

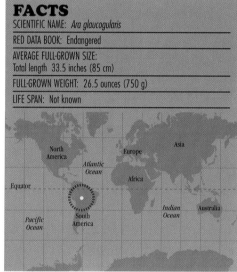

FACTS
SCIENTIFIC NAME: *Ara glaucogularis*

RED DATA BOOK: Endangered

AVERAGE FULL-GROWN SIZE:
Total length 33.5 inches (85 cm)

FULL-GROWN WEIGHT: 26.5 ounces (750 g)

LIFE SPAN: Not known

The blue-throated macaw lives in northern Bolivia.

33

LITTLE BLUE MACAW

FACTS

SCIENTIFIC NAME: *Cyanopsitta spixii*

RED DATA BOOK: Endangered

AVERAGE FULL-GROWN SIZE:
Head and body length 21.7 inches (55 cm)

FULL-GROWN WEIGHT: Male 14 oz. (390 g); female 11.6 oz. (330 g)

LIFE SPAN: Not known

A rare photograph of the only little blue macaw left alive in the wild.

The little blue macaw, or Spix's macaw, is a beautiful parrot that is one of the most endangered birds in the world. There is only one individual left in the wild. The species was originally known only from parrots traded as pets, and the wild population was not found until the 1980s in northern Bahia, Brazil. The parrots were living in gallery forests along the São Francisco River, where they were believed to feed on the fruit of the crabeira tree.

The rarity of the little blue macaw is due to the destruction of its woodland habitat and hunting for the pet trade.

Only four parrots have been found living in the wild. Three of these were believed to have been captured for the illegal parrot trade in 1987 and 1988. Another bird, a male, was discovered in 1990 and is being guarded.

In 1994, thirty-one little blue macaws were known to be held in captivity, with an unknown number undeclared. Twenty-one are captive-bred birds. These parrots are under the control of the Brazilian government's Permanent Committee for the Recovery of Spix's Macaw.

One of the captive females that had been bred in the wild was taken to a large aviary near the home tree of the wild male. The plan is that she will be released and that the pair will eventually mate. Having been kept in a small cage, she must first get used to flying and finding her own food.

Unlike other parrots, even flightless species, the ground parrot has long legs and runs well. It lives along the coast of Australia from Noosa in Queensland through New South Wales and Victoria to South Australia and the southern coast of Western Australia. It also lives in Tasmania and some islands in the Bass Strait. Its habitat lies mainly along the coast or in mountains.

The ground parrot only survives where the heath has not been burned for at least fifteen years. This ensures a rich and diverse vegetation for the birds.

Much of the suitable habitat has been cleared for agriculture and human settlement. As well as being burned, the heath may have also been destroyed by a fungus. The result is that ground parrots are increasingly confined to smaller patches of country. The total numbers are not known, but the western subspecies is down to less than 450.

Ground parrots are nocturnal, and, although they can fly, they spend most of their time on the ground. They feed on seeds and shoots. Their nests are hollows in the ground where the females lay three or four eggs.

Despite the ground parrot's terrestrial way of life, there is no clear evidence that it suffers too much from predators such as foxes and cats. Fire seems to be the main problem, and conservation will depend on research that can show how burning affects the regeneration of the ground parrot's habitat.

FACTS

SCIENTIFIC NAME: *Pezoporus wallicus*

RED DATA BOOK: Endangered

AVERAGE FULL-GROWN SIZE:
Head and body length 3.9 inches (10 cm)
Tail length 7.9 inches (20 cm)

FULL-GROWN WEIGHT: Not known

LIFE SPAN: Not known

The ground parrot has long legs and is an excellent runner. It lives on heaths, and fire is its major threat. When heaths are destroyed, the ground parrot cannot reoccupy the land for fifteen years.

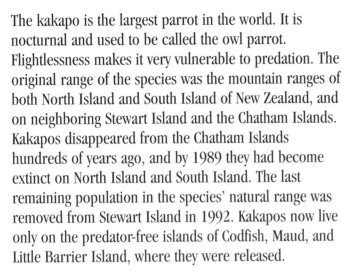

KAKAPO

The kakapo is the largest parrot in the world. It is nocturnal and used to be called the owl parrot. Flightlessness makes it very vulnerable to predation. The original range of the species was the mountain ranges of both North Island and South Island of New Zealand, and on neighboring Stewart Island and the Chatham Islands. Kakapos disappeared from the Chatham Islands hundreds of years ago, and by 1989 they had become extinct on North Island and South Island. The last remaining population in the species' natural range was removed from Stewart Island in 1992. Kakapos now live only on the predator-free islands of Codfish, Maud, and Little Barrier Island, where they were released.

In its original home, the kakapo lived in mossy forests where there are clearings along rivers or in mountain scrub adjoining meadows. It feeds on a variety of plant food, including fruits and nuts, buds and fern roots, fungi, and some animal food. It also chews grass leaves without cutting the plant in order to extract the juices.

Although flightless, kakapos climb trees to eat and glide back to earth. Nests are made among rocks or under tree roots, and females lay three or four eggs.

The kakapo was becoming less common before Europeans arrived in New Zealand, but it disappeared more rapidly afterward. It was hunted for food and killed by introduced rats, weasels, dogs, and other predators. Introduced deer also competed for food.

In 1994, there were only forty-seven kakapos in existence. Seventeen of these were females, and only eight were known breeders. The small number of females and the slow rate of reproduction mean that the kakapo population will take a long time to grow to a safe level. By giving extra food to kakapos on Little Barrier Island, the birds have been persuaded to nest in four out of five years and, in 1991, the first chicks in ten years were reared successfully.

The kakapo, the world's largest parrot, is flightless.

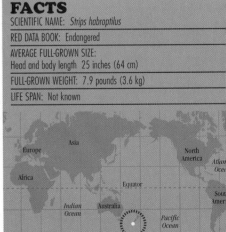

FACTS

SCIENTIFIC NAME: *Strips habroptilus*

RED DATA BOOK: Endangered

AVERAGE FULL-GROWN SIZE:
Head and body length 25 inches (64 cm)

FULL-GROWN WEIGHT: 7.9 pounds (3.6 kg)

LIFE SPAN: Not known

Bannerman's turaco lives in the rain forests of the Bamenda-Banso Highlands of western Cameroon. It plays an important part in the culture of the Kom people. Its feathers are used to decorate the members of the traditional councils, and its song is mimicked by the music of the local xylophone, or njang. The species is still common in the rain forest, but few forests remain.

Nothing is known about the life-style of Bannerman's turaco, except that it seems to be a typical turaco and feeds on fruits and berries.

Survival of Bannerman's turaco depends on preserving its forest home. Clearing the forest for agriculture and grazing cut the species' habitat in half between 1965 and 1985. There are only a few small patches of forest left. The most extensive forest, about 38.5 square miles (100 square kilometers), is on Mount Oku.

A project has been set up on Mount Oku to preserve the forest. Farmers are being taught to use the forest in a sustainable fashion instead of clearing it for agriculture and grazing. One alternative is beekeeping, which needs a healthy forest to provide nectar. Honey brings a good price at local markets.

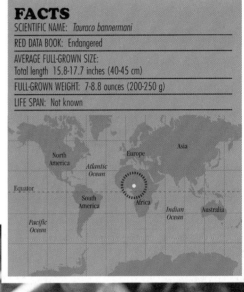

FACTS

SCIENTIFIC NAME: *Tauraco bannermani*

RED DATA BOOK: Endangered

AVERAGE FULL-GROWN SIZE:
Total length 15.8-17.7 inches (40-45 cm)

FULL-GROWN WEIGHT: 7-8.8 ounces (200-250 g)

LIFE SPAN: Not known

Bannerman's turaco can be found around Mount Oku in Cameroon.

FACTS

SCIENTIFIC NAME: *Otus ireneae*

RED DATA BOOK: Endangered

AVERAGE FULL-GROWN SIZE:
Head and body length 6.3-7 inches (16-18 cm)

FULL-GROWN WEIGHT: 1.8 ounces (50 g)

LIFE SPAN: Not known

The Sokoke scops owl was discovered in 1965.

The Sokoke scops owl was discovered only in 1965 when one flew into an ornithologist's net. Since then, only a few specimens have been caught. All were found in the Sokoke Forest Reserve near the coast of Kenya. The species may live elsewhere, however. In 1992, an owl, probably of this species, was found in northern Tanzania. So there is a possibility this elusive bird has a larger range, but the current estimate is that there are about one thousand pairs.

Within Sokoke Forest, the owl has been found in forests and thickets. It eats large insects, such as crickets and katydids, that live on the leaves of trees.

Sokoke Forest is exploited for its valuable timber, but the owl has previously survived this disturbance. However, the forest is now being cleared for plantations, even in the reserve. Preservation of the Sokoke scops owl will depend on proper management of the forest so the owls have somewhere to live while local people have a stock of wood for fuel and other purposes.

BirdLife International has started a major conservation program in Sokoke Forest. There are five other threatened birds besides this owl in the forest, which makes it one of the most important forests requiring preservation in Africa.

This large, spectacular woodpecker used to live in the southeastern United States and in Cuba. Each pair of ivory-billed woodpeckers lived in a large territory of virgin forest. There had to be plenty of old and rotting trees that the woodpeckers could excavate for insects and for nest holes. This means their numbers could never have been very high, and loss of the forests quickly made it impossible for the woodpeckers to survive.

The ivory-billed woodpecker was last seen in the United States in the 1970s. The last known nesting population disappeared in 1948 when an area of Louisiana forest was cleared for growing soybeans. There is, however, a belief that there may be some pairs surviving in some remote area.

The Cuban population dwindled at the same time as that in the United States, but there were sightings in 1988 and possibly even in 1991. As well as destruction of the forest habitat for timber and growing crops, Cuban ivory-billed woodpeckers were also killed so their bodies could be used for personal adornment or to be hung on houses as charms against witchcraft.

There are only two places left in Cuba where the ivory-billed woodpecker could still survive. Although many special expeditions have searched the region where it was last seen, no woodpeckers have been located. A three-month survey of the Ojita de Aqua, where the ivory-billed woodpecker once lived, failed to reveal any definite signs of the species. Neither was there any success in the Sierra Maestra. This is an area of suitable habitat, although it has never been known to support the ivory-billed woodpecker.

The ivory-billed woodpecker may already be extinct in the United States and has not been sighted in Cuba since 1991.

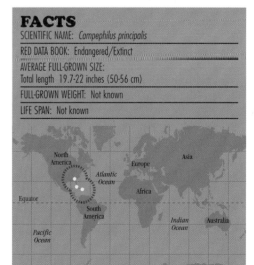

FACTS

SCIENTIFIC NAME: *Campephilus principalis*

RED DATA BOOK: Endangered/Extinct

AVERAGE FULL-GROWN SIZE:
Total length 19.7-22 inches (50-56 cm)

FULL-GROWN WEIGHT: Not known

LIFE SPAN: Not known

The ochraceous attila is a member of the tyrant flycatcher family, the largest and most diverse group of birds in the New World. It lives in the forests of western Ecuador and neighboring parts of Colombia and Peru.

The forests of Ecuador have disappeared rapidly in the last thirty to forty years. In the Celicia Mountains, where most of the ochraceous attilas live, there are very few patches of forest larger than 124 acres (50 ha). The species lives at low densities, so these small fragments of forest do not support viable populations.

Like many small and rare forest birds, the ochraceous attila is not often sighted, and very little is known about its habits. It lives singly or in pairs and does not join the flocks of small birds that are a feature of tropical forests. Its prey consists of insects and spiders, which it catches by picking them from leaves and twigs.

The ochraceous attila lives in some protected areas, but not all the regions are large enough to support a population. The bird's survival will depend on the preservation of sufficiently large areas of forest.

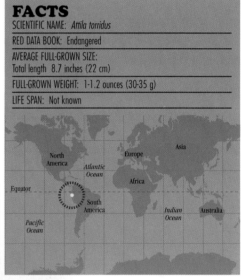

FACTS

SCIENTIFIC NAME: *Attila torridus*

RED DATA BOOK: Endangered

AVERAGE FULL-GROWN SIZE:
Total length 8.7 inches (22 cm)

FULL-GROWN WEIGHT: 1-1.2 ounces (30-35 g)

LIFE SPAN: Not known

The survival of the ochraceous attila depends on the preservation of its forest habitat.

FACTS

SCIENTIFIC NAME: *Pitta gurneyi*

RED DATA BOOK: Endangered

AVERAGE FULL-GROWN SIZE:
Total length 7.9 inches (20 cm)

FULL-GROWN WEIGHT: 3.5-3.9 ounces (100-110 g)

LIFE SPAN: Not known

Gurney's pitta is close to extinction.

Fifty to one hundred years ago, Gurney's pitta was a common bird in the lowland rain forests of Thailand and Myanmar. It is now close to extinction in Thailand, and it has not been recorded in Myanmar since 1914.

Gurney's pitta lives on the ground. Even when disturbed, it escapes by hopping or flying for short distances near the ground. It feeds by turning leaves with its beak and searching for earthworms, snails, and insects with its acute sense of smell.

Survival is impossible without the rain forest, and the lowland forests have almost disappeared. Bird catchers are another threat, and remaining populations are hard to find. Six years of searching by local ornithologists in Trang Province of Thailand was rewarded in 1986 when they found a nesting pair. The only viable population was found during another survey in Krabi Province, where experts estimated twenty-four to thirty-four pairs.

A conservation project is trying to save the habitat of the Krabi Province population by persuading local people to keep pigs instead of hunting in the forest. They are also given native trees to plant, including species the Gurney's pitta uses for nesting. Guard patrols prevent trapping of the birds. The result is that local people have learned they have a very special bird living in their neighborhood and that saving Gurney's pitta will bring them economic benefit.

FACTS

SCIENTIFIC NAME: *Atrichornis clamosus*

RED DATA BOOK: Endangered

AVERAGE FULL-GROWN SIZE:
Head and body length 8.3 inches (21 cm)
Tail length 3.9 inches (10 cm)

FULL-GROWN WEIGHT: Not known

LIFE SPAN: Not known

The noisy scrub bird lives in dense eucalyptus forests in Australia.

The noisy scrub bird gets its name from its repertoire of loud whistles and trills. It is one of two scrub bird species. The other is the rufous scrub bird, which is also threatened. After it had been seen in 1899, the noisy scrub bird was not recorded again until 1961.

The original home of the noisy scrub bird was a large area of southwestern Australia that was covered with dense eucalyptus forests. Fires lit by European settlers to clear the land destroyed the noisy scrub bird's habitat and killed the large insects, such as crickets and cockroaches, that it ate.

By 1976, the noisy scrub bird's range had shrunk to the Mount Gardener area of the Two Peoples Bay Nature Reserve, 25 miles (40 kilometers) east of Albany. This area has not been burned like the surrounding country because of the difficult nature of the terrain. With the aid of a conservation program, the noisy scrub bird's range is increasing again. In 1993, a survey showed there were about four hundred males holding territories and singing.

Noisy scrub birds do not fly well; they prefer to run through the undergrowth when disturbed. They lay only one egg a year, so they are vulnerable to predators.

The noisy scrub bird was rediscovered in 1961 in an area that was planned for a new town. These plans were abandoned, and the area was turned into a nature reserve. Some birds have been taken to new areas to help the population expand. Survival depends on preserving areas of habitat large enough to hold viable populations.

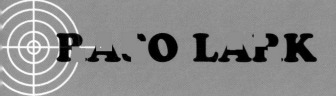
The Raso lark is a type of skylark that lives only on the small, uninhabited island of Raso in the Cape Verde Islands. The larks used to live in the central part of the island, which is only 2.7 sq. miles (7 sq. km) in area, but they are now found only in the southwestern section. The habitat is level plains of volcanic soil with low, sparse vegetation.

Raso larks live in flocks outside the nesting season. Their food is probably insects and seeds. Their nests are built in low vegetation, and females lay three eggs.

Until 1963, the species was abundant in its small area of habitat. Since then, numbers have dropped, and only fifteen to twenty larks were found in 1981. This was probably due to several years of drought that affected the island's vegetation and left the larks short of food. Numbers have increased again to about 250 birds.

If the species does not become extinct through natural causes, such as drought, the main threat to the Raso lark is introduced predators. There are no human inhabitants on the island at this time, but settlers might bring rats or other animals. In 1994, a dog was found on the island.

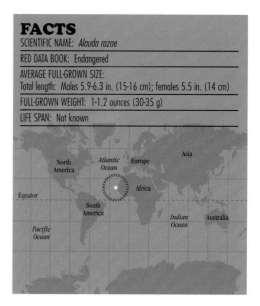

FACTS

SCIENTIFIC NAME: *Alauda razae*

RED DATA BOOK: Endangered

AVERAGE FULL-GROWN SIZE:
Total length: Males 5.9-6.3 in. (15-16 cm); females 5.5 in. (14 cm)

FULL-GROWN WEIGHT: 1-1.2 ounces (30-35 g)

LIFE SPAN: Not known

Since 1981, the Raso lark population has increased from about 15 or 20 birds to about 250 birds.

FACTS

SCIENTIFIC NAME: *Nesomimus trifasciatus*

RED DATA BOOK: Endangered

AVERAGE FULL-GROWN SIZE:
Total length 9.9 inches (25 cm)

FULL-GROWN WEIGHT: Male 2.3 oz. (66 g); female 2.1 oz. (60 g)

LIFE SPAN: Not known

Rats and disease are the greatest threats to the survival of the Charles mockingbird.

There are four species of mockingbirds living on the Galápagos Islands. The Charles mockingbird lives on two islands – Champion and Gardner. It used to live on a third – Floreana, once called Charles. It was common on Floreana, but it was last seen there in 1868. By 1888, it had become extinct. There are still two hundred to three hundred birds on Champion and about fifty on Gardner.

The Charles mockingbird lives in flocks of four to ten birds. It feeds on the ground, hunting insects and crabs, taking fruit from trees and bushes, and stealing eggs from other birds and reptiles. Females lay two to five eggs; several members of the flock help raise the young.

Rats, which were introduced in the 1830s, caused the extinction of the Charles mockingbird on Floreana. The species will survive on Champion and Gardner only if rats are kept off the islands.

The small size of the two remaining populations means they could be easily wiped out by a natural disaster. Every few years, there is a change in the Galápagos Islands to cold, wet weather. This is caused by a sea current called El Niño that affects the climate. In these conditions, there are outbreaks of avian pox, a fatal disease. The Charles mockingbird could become extinct if some other disaster struck after an epidemic of avian pox.

The Rodriguez brush-warbler is restricted to Rodriguez, a small island that lies 342 miles (550 km) east of Mauritius in the Indian Ocean. It once lived all over the island, but in 1974 there were only twenty to twenty-five pairs left, and a cyclone in 1979 reduced these to four pairs and a single bird.

The original habitat of the Rodriguez brush-warbler was the native forest and scrub, but it adapted to plantations of introduced trees and shrubs such as mahogany, guava, and jamrose. The species is insectivorous and feeds by picking insects off leaves and twigs. Females lay a clutch of three eggs, but usually only one young bird is reared.

The main threats to the Rodriguez brush-warbler are the destruction of vegetation for fuel or grazing and damage caused by cyclones. The introduced vegetation is not as resistant to fierce winds as the native plants. When the population is low, cyclones can have a devastating effect, and Cyclone Monique in 1968 nearly wiped out the species. The ship, or black, rat colonized Rodriguez in the 1980s, and there are fears that this nest predator will prevent the recovery of the brush-warbler population. Similarly, monkeys brought to the island as pets may escape and prey on the brush-warblers.

Replanting the island's vegetation cover, especially after cyclones, is the main way to conserve the Rodriguez brush-warbler. The population had increased to somewhere between 45 and 65 birds in 1991 and is now stable, although the species still needs guarding.

The Rodriguez brush-warbler is under constant threat from habitat destruction, natural disasters, and rats.

FACTS

SCIENTIFIC NAME: *Bebrornis rodericanus*

RED DATA BOOK: Endangered

AVERAGE FULL-GROWN SIZE:
Total length 5.9 inches (15 cm)

FULL-GROWN WEIGHT: Not known

LIFE SPAN: Not known

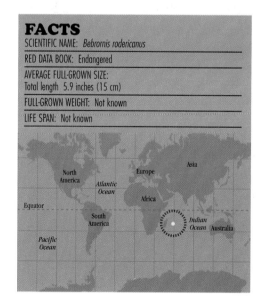

The eight species of magpie-robins live in Africa and Asia. The Seychelles magpie-robin lives only on the Seychelles Islands, and its population once dropped to fewer than fifteen birds.

The original home of the Seychelles magpie-robin was in the forests that covered the Seychelles Islands. The birds need open ground under the trees so they can search for small animals, such as earthworms, centipedes, scorpions, and insects. Sometimes they eat small reptiles and amphibians. They follow large animals, such as tortoises and pigs, to catch the small animals they disturb. Their nests are cups of dry grass and coconut fiber. Females lay a single egg.

At one time, the Seychelles magpie-robin lived in the forests on many of the Seychelles Islands, but, since human settlers arrived in 1770, the people have cleared the forests. The Seychelles magpie-robin became extinct on the largest island, Mahé, by 1880. Introduced cats and rats also contributed to its decline.

The Seychelles magpie-robin survived only on the island of Frégate, but it has since been reintroduced to Aride. A program to help the species was organized in 1988. The habitat has been improved by clearing scrub and planting native trees. Cats have been removed and the numbers of the common myna reduced. The magpie-robins have also been helped by being provided with extra nesting sites and food and by having nest protection. The result has been a large increase in numbers, and the plan is to establish a population of eighty to one hundred birds.

FACTS

SCIENTIFIC NAME:	*Copsychus sechellarum*
RED DATA BOOK:	Endangered
AVERAGE FULL-GROWN SIZE: Head and body length 9.9 inches (25 cm)	
FULL-GROWN WEIGHT:	Not known
LIFE SPAN:	14 years

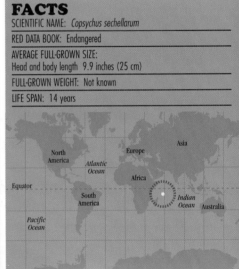

The Seychelles magpie-robin survives in small numbers on two of the Seychelles Islands.

FACTS

SCIENTIFIC NAME: *Petroica traversi*

RED DATA BOOK: Endangered

AVERAGE FULL-GROWN SIZE:
Head and body length 5.9 inches (15 cm)

FULL-GROWN WEIGHT: .8 ounces (23 g)

LIFE SPAN: 12 years

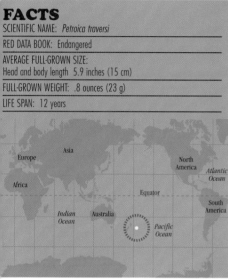

The Chatham robin was saved by a successful breeding campaign that raised its numbers from 5 in 1980 to 100 by 1988.

The Chatham robin, once known as the Chatham Island black robin, lives only on the Chatham Islands group, 560 miles (900 km) east of the coast of South Island in New Zealand. It has relatives living elsewhere in Australasia. It feeds on insects and other invertebrate animals and lays two or three eggs.

When Europeans colonized the Chatham Islands, the robin quickly disappeared. The forest habitat was destroyed by grazing animals, and predators were introduced. By 1880, the robin was restricted to a single island, Little Mangere Island.

When the habitat on Little Mangere Island was destroyed by wild sheep, the remaining population of seven robins was transferred to Mangere Island. By 1980, only five were left, and these included just one breeding pair.

The Chatham robin has been saved by humans who help it produce more young. Experts once thought a pair could lay only two or three eggs. However, if these are removed, the birds lay more. Therefore, eggs have been taken from robin nests and put in the nests of the Chatham Island tit and the Chatham Island warbler, where they are successfully reared by their foster parents. The robin pair then rears another family.

Chatham robin nests are also protected from starlings and other birds by placing them in nest boxes. The number of young reared is also increased by dusting the nests with insecticide to kill fleas and mites that harm the nestlings. In 1988, the population had risen to one hundred birds.

FACTS

SCIENTIFIC NAME:	*Platysteira laticincta*
RED DATA BOOK:	Endangered
AVERAGE FULL-GROWN SIZE:	Total length 5.5 inches (14 cm)
FULL-GROWN WEIGHT:	.4-.5 ounces (12-15 g)
LIFE SPAN:	Not known

The banded wattle-eye is a solitary bird that lives only in western Cameroon.

The banded wattle-eye is a flycatcher that lives only in the Bamenda-Banso Highlands in western Cameroon. It was discovered in 1925 and will become extinct if the montane forests in this region disappear.

Very little is known about the habits of the banded wattle-eye except that it is solitary and hunts insects.

The rising human population is steadily destroying the forests of Cameroon. Even the surviving fragments are being altered as people cultivate crops under the trees, cut firewood, and graze their animals. As the natural vegetation is removed, the soil becomes eroded, and regeneration of the forest becomes impossible.

Several endangered bird species live in the Bamenda-Banso Highlands, including Bannerman's turaco. They will become extinct when the forest disappears. Two conservation projects are working to help save the remaining forests. They are helping the local people to find alternative ways of making a living without destroying the forest. Representatives of the Cameroon government and farmers meet to agree on a plan for each part of the forest. Beekeeping and selling honey is one way of making use of the forest resources without destroying it.

An artist's impression of the rare Kauai oo bird of Hawaii.

The Kauai oo is a member of the very varied family of Hawaiian honeycreepers. It used to be common in forests that covered the island of Kauai, but it became very rare and was thought to be extinct. The Kauai oo was found again in 1960 living in the Alakai swamp, but only a few individuals are known to survive.

Little is known about the habits of the Kauai oo, but it lives like a woodpecker. It climbs the trunks of trees and searches for insects and spiders in the bark. It nests in a hole in a tree trunk.

Destruction of the forests and diseases carried by introduced mosquitoes probably caused the decline of the Kauai oo. It was probably saved from extinction by its dull plumage, which meant that it was not hunted by Hawaiians for its feathers.

The Alakai swamp is now part of a wilderness reserve where the forest habitat is being preserved to help forest birds. However, this may not be enough to save the Kauai oo from extinction.

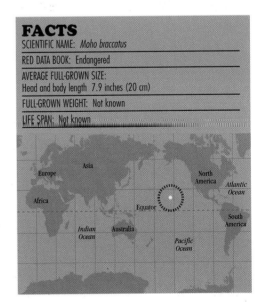

FACTS

SCIENTIFIC NAME: *Moho braccatus*

RED DATA BOOK: Endangered

AVERAGE FULL-GROWN SIZE:
Head and body length 7.9 inches (20 cm)

FULL-GROWN WEIGHT: Not known

LIFE SPAN: Not known

Kirtland's warbler lives only in parts of Michigan and Wisconsin in the United States, with occasional pairs nesting in Ontario and Quebec in Canada. Most of the breeding pairs are in the two counties of Oscoda and Crawford in Michigan. Their winter home is in the Bahama Islands and the Turks and Caicos Islands.

This species has very special habitat requirements. It nests only in young jack pines growing in sandy soil. The trees must be growing in uniform stands about 6.6 to 13 feet (2 to 4 m) high and about eight to twenty years old. There were originally about 247,100 acres (100,000 ha) of jack pine forest, but Kirtland's warbler could use only a small part where the trees were the right height, about 9,885 acres (4,000 ha), at any time. Areas of trees at the right height used to be created by natural fires, but forest management has reduced the number and size of fires and replaced jack pines with other species of trees. As a result, the population of Kirtland's warbler dropped from 502 singing males in 1961 to 167 in 1974.

The breeding success of the surviving Kirtland's warblers is reduced by the brown-headed cowbird that lays its eggs in the warblers' nests. At one point, cowbird numbers increased until about two-thirds of Kirtland's warbler nests were being taken over each year.

Conservation of the Kirtland's warbler involves burning areas of jack pine forest to allow regrowth of uniform stands and the planting of new trees (1.3 million in 1991). The cowbird problem is also being addressed. The result is that pairs of Kirtland's warblers are rearing more than four young per nest, the highest for any American warbler, and the number of singing males increased to 633 by 1994. In the same year, the first Kirtland's Warbler Festival, a ten-day event, was held in Oscoda County, Michigan.

Kirtland's warbler has been the subject of a successful breeding campaign in Michigan.

FACTS

SCIENTIFIC NAME:	*Dendroica kirtlandii*
RED DATA BOOK:	Endangered
AVERAGE FULL-GROWN SIZE: Total length 5.9 inches (15 cm)	
FULL-GROWN WEIGHT:	.4-.6 ounces (12.2-16 g)
LIFE SPAN:	Not known

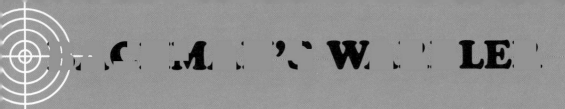

Bachman's warbler may be extinct. It was last seen in August 1988, and the last nest was found in 1937.

Until the start of the twentieth century, Bachman's warbler was common in many parts of Missouri, Arkansas, Kentucky, Alabama, and South Carolina. It spent summers nesting in canebrakes of bamboo growing in river swamps that flooded for part of the year. It migrated through Florida and wintered in Cuba. The canebrakes have virtually disappeared through drainage for cultivation and flood control. The forests where the warblers spent winters in Cuba have been replaced almost entirely by sugarcane. Shooting by collectors has also hastened the disappearance of Bachman's warbler. One hundred and ninety-two birds were shot by American collectors between 1886 and 1892.

Very little is known about the habits of Bachman's warbler, but conservationists do know that it nested in dense foliage high in trees, and females laid three eggs.

Recent searches have been made for Bachman's warbler without success. If it still exists, it will probably be in the l'On Swamp area of South Carolina, which is now within the Francis Marion National Forest.

Bachman's warbler may already be extinct. If not, it remains well hidden in the swamps of South Carolina.

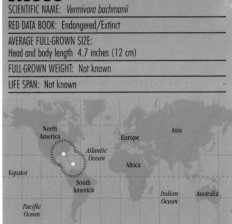

FACTS

SCIENTIFIC NAME: *Vermivora bachmanii*

RED DATA BOOK: Endangered/Extinct

AVERAGE FULL-GROWN SIZE:
Head and body length 4.7 inches (12 cm)

FULL-GROWN WEIGHT: Not known

LIFE SPAN: Not known

The ou is one of the largest Hawaiian honeycreepers. It was once common in forests on six of the Hawaiian islands, including Hawaii itself. Its habitat was mainly wet forests, and it was recently found in forests of ohia and koa trees. It is now so rare and difficult to find that very little is known of its habits.

Much of Hawaii's forests have been destroyed. The most common native tree, the ohia, has died back, for unknown reasons, on the island of Hawaii. A lava flow from the volcano Mauna Loa destroyed some of the habitat in 1984.

Introduced diseases carried by mosquitoes have killed ous. Other introduced insects have driven out some of the native insects the ous used as food.

Conservationists believe there may be a few hundred ous alive, but only two were found in a survey made in 1989. None have been seen since Hurricane Iniki in 1992. The ou only has a chance of survival if its habitat can be saved. In 1985, over 7,415 acres (3,000 ha) of native forest were purchased on the island of Hawaii to form the basis of a reserve. The area, known as the Hakalau Forest National Wildlife Refuge, is now five times larger and contains koa and ohia forests.

An artist's impression of the ou, which lives only in Hawaii. There have been no sightings of the bird since its habitat was affected by a hurricane in 1992.

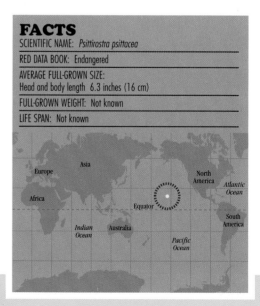

FACTS

SCIENTIFIC NAME: *Psittirostra psittacea*

RED DATA BOOK: Endangered

AVERAGE FULL-GROWN SIZE:
Head and body length 6.3 inches (16 cm)

FULL-GROWN WEIGHT: Not known

LIFE SPAN: Not known

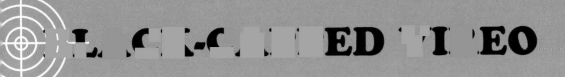

The black-capped vireo was plentiful at one time, with a large breeding range from Kansas through Oklahoma and Texas to Coahuila in Mexico. The species is migratory and spends winters on the Pacific coast of Mexico. Its breeding habitat is the border between woodland and grassland where there are scattered thickets of trees and shrubs along ridges and gulleys.

Black-capped vireos feed mainly on insects, but they also eat fruit when in season. Their nests are suspended from the fork of a branch. Females lay four or five eggs.

Like several other species, the black-capped vireo suffers from nest parasitism by the brown-headed cowbird. The cowbird lays its own eggs in the nests of black-capped vireos or other species and destroys their eggs. This has happened for millions of years, but in recent times cowbirds have become more abundant and have increased their range. The change is due to the loss of wooded country to agriculture, which improves the habitat for cowbirds. In some places, black-capped vireos lose nine out of ten clutches to cowbirds.

Black-capped vireos are now found only in a few places in Oklahoma, Texas, and Coahuila. The total population is less than two thousand birds.

A National Wildlife Refuge has been set up for the black-capped vireo near Austin, Texas. Experts plan to help the species by reducing the threat from cowbirds.

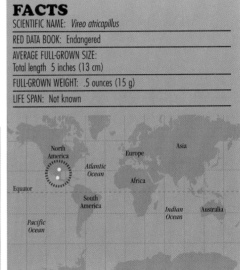

FACTS

SCIENTIFIC NAME: *Vireo atricapillus*

RED DATA BOOK: Endangered

AVERAGE FULL-GROWN SIZE:
Total length 5 inches (13 cm)

FULL-GROWN WEIGHT: .5 ounces (15 g)

LIFE SPAN: Not known

The black-capped vireo is one of many bird species threatened by the nest parasitism of cowbirds.

The Martinique oriole is the only species of bird that lives on the island of Martinique and nowhere else. It is also unusual because humans are not to blame for its endangered status. It used to be found throughout the island and lived in a variety of habitats from mangroves to wooded gardens, but it has disappeared from many areas in the last fifty years.

The Martinique oriole feeds in the canopy of trees, eating fruit and insects. Its nest hangs from a leaf, and the females lay three eggs.

The decline of the Martinique oriole was caused by the shiny cowbird. Like other cowbird species, this bird is a nest parasite. It lays its eggs in the nests of other birds. The host birds' eggs are destroyed or, if they hatch, the young cowbird takes most of the food so the hosts' nestlings starve.

The shiny cowbird originated in South America, and it has been spreading naturally through the West Indies. It arrived on Martinique in the 1940s and now parasitizes nearly two-thirds of all Martinique oriole nests. There is very little that can be done about this except for killing the cowbirds. However, there has been a natural decline in cowbirds recently, thereby allowing a rise in the numbers of Martinique orioles.

FACTS

SCIENTIFIC NAME: *Icterus bonana*

RED DATA BOOK: Endangered

AVERAGE FULL-GROWN SIZE:
Total length 7.9 inches (20 cm)

FULL-GROWN WEIGHT: 1.2 ounces (35 g)

LIFE SPAN: Not known

The Martinique oriole lives only on the island and is endangered because of parasitic cowbirds.

RED SISKIN

FACTS

SCIENTIFIC NAME: *Carduelis cucullata*

RED DATA BOOK: Endangered

AVERAGE FULL-GROWN SIZE:
Head and body length 3.9 inches (10 cm)

FULL-GROWN WEIGHT: Not known

LIFE SPAN: Not known

The greatest threat to red siskins is their popularity for the cage bird market.

The red siskin lives mainly in northern Venezuela with small numbers in northeastern Colombia. There is also a small population in Puerto Rico; these siskins are descended from birds that escaped from captivity. Red siskins once lived on Trinidad, but the species is now extinct there. The habitat is open forests and forest edges, where flocks of red siskins search for food and water. They eat a variety of fruit and seeds.

Although the habitat of the red siskin has been disappearing, the main threat has been collection for sale. For over one hundred years, red siskins have been trapped for the cage bird trade and at one time for their feathers, which were used in ladies' hats. The red siskin is very popular as a cage bird because it interbreeds with the canary. The offspring are fertile and have a reddish plumage. They are also very good singers. More red siskins were trapped than were needed for sale, however, so there was a high mortality rate.

The trade in red siskins was banned in Venezuela fifty years ago, but an illegal trade continues to thrive. New roads allow trappers to reach the breeding areas at any time of year, and ten years ago a single red siskin was worth $10,000.

The red siskin's wild population will survive only if it can be saved from trappers and if enough birds can be bred in captivity to meet the demand for cage birds.

The Bali myna is a relative of the Indian hill myna, which is well known as a cage bird and a good mimic. It is found only on the island of Bali, in Indonesia. It used to range across the western third of the island but is now confined to the extreme northwestern tip.

The habitat of the Bali myna is forest and acacia savanna. It needs holes in trees, usually old woodpecker holes, for nesting. It feeds on insects, such as caterpillars, ants, and termites. When still abundant, it lived in flocks of up to forty birds.

In addition to the destruction of its limited habitat, the Bali myna has suffered from competition with the black-winged starling for nest holes. The main threat today is capture for the cage bird trade. Although fully protected by Indonesian law, illegal capture continues. As the Bali myna becomes rarer, the price for a bird increases, which encourages more poaching. In 1990, the wild population was probably as few as thirteen birds.

The present range of the Bali myna lies within the Bali Barat National Park; the Bali Starling (Myna) Project was launched in 1987 to improve guarding of the park. There are around seven hundred Bali mynas in captivity, and the release of their offpsring has raised the population in the wild to somewhere between thirty-five to fifty-five. Although the free-living birds nested well in 1993, there was no increase in the population. This shows they are still being captured. The population in 1994 was approximately thirty-six to forty birds.

FACTS

SCIENTIFIC NAME: *Leucopsar rothschildi*

RED DATA BOOK: Endangered

AVERAGE FULL-GROWN SIZE:
Total length 9.9 inches (25 cm)

FULL-GROWN WEIGHT: 3-3.2 ounces (85-90 g)

LIFE SPAN: Not known

The Bali myna's greatest enemy is its beauty, which makes it popular with cage bird traders.

The kokako is a member of the New Zealand wattlebird family. Its habitat is the native lowland forests, and it could once be found throughout New Zealand, including Stewart Island and the Great Barrier Islands. Loss of the native forest is probably the main cause for the kokako's endangered status.

The kokako does not fly well, and it moves around by hopping on its long legs. When in trees, it hops from branch to branch and occasionally glides from one tree to another. The kokako's weak flight makes it vulnerable to predators. Its main food is fruit, and it makes a large, untidy nest high in a tree, where it lays two or three eggs.

There are two subspecies of kokako, one on South Island and one on North Island. The one living on South Island was once believed to be extinct, but it may still occur on Stewart Island. The North Island subspecies numbers about 1,500 to 2,000.

The kokako is legally protected, and several reserves have been created for it. Some birds have been moved to Little Barrier and Kapiti islands, where they are safe from predators.

A flightless bird, the kokako hops through the branches of trees in New Zealand.

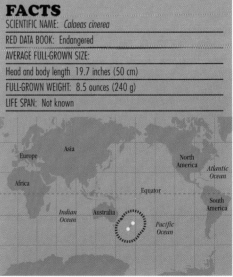

FACTS

SCIENTIFIC NAME:	*Calaeas cinerea*
RED DATA BOOK:	Endangered
AVERAGE FULL-GROWN SIZE:	
Head and body length	19.7 inches (50 cm)
FULL-GROWN WEIGHT:	8.5 ounces (240 g)
LIFE SPAN:	Not known

HAWAIIAN CROW

FACTS

SCIENTIFIC NAME: *Corvus hawaiiensis*

RED DATA BOOK: Endangered

AVERAGE FULL-GROWN SIZE:
Total length 18.9 inches (48 cm)

FULL-GROWN WEIGHT: Not known

LIFE SPAN: Not known

The entire population of the rare Hawaiian crow lives on one ranch and numbers fewer than forty birds.

Like many of the unique species of birds living on the Hawaiian Islands, the Hawaiian crow is in danger of extinction from the impact of human settlement. Large numbers of specialized birds evolved on this island group, but their numbers were never very high, and they had no defense against introduced predators or changes to their habitat. Hawaiian crows were always restricted to the main island of Hawaii, and they nested only on the forested slopes of Hualalai and Mauna Loa volcanoes.

The Hawaiian crow is fairly tame. It eats mainly fruit, but also searches for ground insects and flower nectar. It lays from one to five eggs, but breeding success is poor.

The Hawaiian crow was common until the 1930s. Its disappearance was due to a combination of habitat destruction, introduced predators, and perhaps disease. More recently, it has been hunted illegally. There are now only thirty-one to thirty-six birds in the wild and in captivity.

Survival of the Hawaiian crow will probably depend on captive breeding, although it is not easy to persuade it to breed. The first successful hatching and fledging in captivity was in 1988 at the Olinda Endangered Species Breeding Facility on the island of Maui. In 1994, there were nine captive-reared chicks, and seven of these were being prepared for release into the wild.

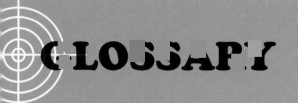

amphibians — cold-blooded animals that live both in water and on land.

aquatic — living in water.

arboreal — living in trees.

ban — to deny or prohibit.

birds — warm-blooded animals that lay eggs and have feathers and wings.

breed — to mate a male and female animal for the purpose of producing offspring.

canopy — the uppermost layer of a forest.

carnivores — flesh-eating animals.

carrion — the dead, often rotting, flesh of animals used as food by other animals.

colonies — groups of animals or plants of the same kind living together.

conservation — the act of preserving animals, plants, or other resources from extinction.

crustaceans — invertebrate animals with segmented bodies and external skeletons or shells. Shrimp and crabs are crustaceans.

drought — an extended period of time when there is very little or no rainfall.

endangered — at risk of dying out completely, or becoming extinct.

evergreen — plants with leaves or needles that stay green throughout the year.

expeditions — journeys made to accomplish a mission or specific goal.

extinct — no longer existing or living.

floodplain — low or level land adjoining a river or other body of water that is likely to flood because of heavy rains, melting snow, etc.

habitat — the natural home of an animal or plant.

herds — animals of the same type that live together in groups.

insectivorous — eating insects for food.

invertebrates — animals such as worms, clams, and insects that do not have a backbone.

larva — the wingless, wormlike form of a newly hatched insect. The larva is the stage of development that appears after the egg but before adulthood; e.g., a caterpillar is the larva of the butterfly or moth.

maize — the corn plant.

mammals — warm-blooded animals that feed their young with mother's milk.

mangrove — a tropical tree that lives in a waterlogged, salty environment.

marshes — waterlogged ground; swampy land.

mate — (n) the male or female of a pair of animals; (v) when animals join together for the purpose of producing offspring.

migration — the movement of animals from one environment to another, often over long distances and usually following certain routes on a seasonal basis.

mollusks — invertebrate animals, such as clams and snails, with an unsegmented body and a hard shell.

monogamous — having only one mate at a time.

native — originating or occurring naturally in a region or other particular place.

nocturnal — active only during the night.

ornithologists — scientists who study birds.

oxides — compounds of oxygen and another element.

pastures — grassland areas suitable for grazing livestock.

persecute — to oppress or cause suffering to a particular group.

pesticides — toxic chemicals used to kill insects.

plantations — large estates that grow a single crop.

plateau — an area of flat land that is higher in elevation than the land surrounding it.

poaching — the illegal catching of animals, usually for profit.

pollution — impure, or dirty, air, water, and land.

prairie — a grassy plain with no trees.

predators — animals that feed by catching and eating other animals.

prey — animals that are eaten by other animals.

ravines — narrow, deep valleys.

remote — removed from the main traffic routes.

reptiles — cold-blooded animals with scaly skins; e.g., snakes, lizards, crocodiles, and tortoises.

reserves — areas of land set aside for the protection of wildlife.

reservoir — an area where water has been collected for a certain use.

roost — a perch or other place where birds rest. Also the name for a group of resting birds.

sanctuaries — areas where animals can live protected from harm.

savanna — an environment of grassy plains with clumps of trees.

scavengers — animals that feed on dead animals and plants.

scrub — vegetation consisting of stunted trees and shrubs.

smuggling — the practice of taking an object out of a country illegally and secretly.

spawning ground — an area where large numbers of fish lay their eggs.

species — a group of animals or plants that breeds with each other, but does not breed with animals or plants outside the group.

spores — single animal or plant cells that can grow into a new animal or plant.

swamp — an area of muddy land that is often filled with water.

tropical — of or relating to the warm, humid area of Earth near the equator. The tropics are the areas of our planet that lie between the Tropic of Cancer and the Tropic of Capricorn.

vertebrates — animals that have a backbone.

viable — (a population) large enough to continue breeding and existing.

waders — long-legged birds that wade rather than swim in marshes, lakes, or rivers.

All Wild Creatures Welcome: The Story of a Wildlife Rehabilitation Center. Patricia Curtis (Lodestar)
The Californian Wildlife Region. V. Brown and G. Lawrence (Naturegraph)
Close to Extinction. John Burton (Watts)
Conservation Directory. (National Wildlife Federation)
Conservation from A to Z. I. Green (Oddo)
Discovering Birds of Prey. Mike Thomas and Eric Soothill (Watts)
Discovering Endangered Species (Nature Discovery Library). Nancy Field and Sally Machlas
   (Dog Eared Publications)
Ecology Basics. Lawrence Stevens (Prentice Hall)
Endangered Animals. John B. Wexo (Creative Education)
Endangered Forest Animals. Dave Taylor (Crabtree)
Endangered Grassland Animals. Dave Taylor (Crabtree)
Endangered Mountain Animals. Dave Taylor (Crabtree)
Endangered Wetland Animals. Dave Taylor (Crabtree)
Endangered Species. Don Lynch (Grace Dangberg Foundation)
Endangered Species Means There's Still Time. (U.S. Government Printing Office, Washington, D.C.)
Endangered Wildlife. M. Banks (Rourke)
Fifty Simple Things Kids Can Do to Save the Earth. Earthworks Group (Andrews and McMeel)
Heroes of Conservation. C. B. Squire (Fleet)
In Peril (4 volumes). Barbara J. Behm and Jean-Christophe Balouet (Gareth Stevens)
Lost Wide Worlds. Robert M. McClung (William Morrow)
Macmillan Children's Guide to Endangered Animals. Roger Few (Macmillan)
Meant to Be Wild. Jan DeBlieu (Fulcrum)
Mountain Gorillas in Danger. Rita Ritchie (Gareth Stevens)
National Wildlife Federation's Book of Endangered Species. Earthbooks, Inc. Staff (Earthbooks, Inc.)
Project Panda Watch. Miriam Schlein (Atheneum)
Save the Earth. Betty Miles (Knopf)
Saving Animals: The World Wildlife Book of Conservation. Bernard Stonehouse (Macmillan)
Why Are Animals Endangered? Isaac Asimov (Gareth Stevens)
Wildlife Alert. Gene S. Stuart (National Geographic)
Wildlife of Cactus and Canyon Country. Marjorie Dunmire (Pegasus)
Wildlife of the Northern Rocky Mountains. William Baker (Naturegraph)

VIDEOS

African Wildlife. (National Geographic)
The Amazing Marsupials. (National Geographic)
Animals Are Beautiful People. Jamie Uys (Pro Footage Library: America's Wildlife)
How to Save Planet Earth. (Pro Footage Library: America's Wildlife)
Predators of the Wild. (Time Warner Entertainment)
Wildlife of Alaska. (Pro Footage Library: America's Wildlife)

INDEX

PICTURE CREDITS

Front cover, @ Tim Laman/The Wildlife
   Collection
Page 9, Javier Barrio/BirdLife International;
Pages 10, 43, 48, BirdLife International;
Page 11, M.P. Kahl/VIREO;
Page 12, Udo Hirsch/WWF;
Pages 13, 16, 27, 35, 49, 52, 57, Paul
   Barruel/WWF;
Page14, Olivier Langrand/WWF;
Page 15, A & E Morris/VIREO;
Page 17, Joseph Van Wormer/Bruce Coleman
   Ltd;
Page 18, Wolfgang Salb/Free Ltd/WWF;
Page 19, 28, Michael Brooke;
Page 20, J.D. Bland/VIREO;
Page 21, P.J. Garson/BirdLife International;
Page 22, Jeff Foott Productions/Bruce Coleman
   Ltd;
Pages 23, 36, Gerald Cubitt/Bruce Coleman Ltd;
Page 24, Christian Zuber/Bruce Coleman Ltd;
Pages 25, 26, 47, B. Chudleigh/VIREO;
Page 28, Brian Coates/Bruce Coleman Ltd;
Page 30, Rod Williams/Bruce Coleman Ltd;

Page 31, Michel Gunther/BIOS/WWF;
Page 32, Michael Rothman/WWF;
Page 33, Dieter Hoppe/BirdLife International;
Pages 34, 38, Luiz Claudio Marigo/Bruce
   Coleman Ltd;
Pages 37, 48, J. Parrott/BirdLife International;
Page 39, C.C. Lockwood/Animals
   Animals/Oxford Scientific Films;
Page 40, R. Ridbely/VIREO;
Page 41, Philip D. Round/WWF;
Page 42, Babs & Bert Wells/Oxford Scientific
   Films;
Page 44, V.-J. Rey-Millet/WWF;
Page 45, A. Forbes-Watson/VIREO;
Page 46, Jack Stein Grove, Eye on the
   World/WWF;
Page 50, Dan Roby/VIREO;
Page 51, J.H. Dick/VIREO;
Page 53, M. Lockwood/VIREO;
Page 54, Doug Wechsler/VIREO;
Page 55, Hans Reinhard/Bruce Coleman Ltd;
Page 56, Alain Compost/WWF;

Page 58, Paul Banko/Hawaii Volcanoes National
   Park/ BirdLife International

WWF = World Wide Fund for Nature